Ketogenic Bread

Best Low Carb Recipes for Ketogenic Gluten Free and Paleo Diets. Keto Loaves, Snacks, Cookies, Muffins, Buns for Rapid Weight Loss and A Healthy Lifestyle.

Valerie Dave

INTRODUCTION

Low Carb Bread Recipes

Quick Radish Chips

Eggs Free Gluten Free Pumpkin Cookies

No Egg Coconut Flour Cookies

Low Carb Keto Hazelnut Flour Cookies

Low Carb Cranberry Walnut Cookies

Gluten Free -Cranberry Biscotti Cookies

Keto Low Carb Hamburger Buns

Keto, Paleo Low Carb Hamburger Buns Recipe

Low Carb Keto Bread

Small Chocolate Chip Muffins with Peanut Butter

Low Carb Gluten Free -Garlic Coconut Flour Bagels

Gluten Free -French Toast Bagels

Fancy Carrot Cake Cream Cheese Muffins- Low Carb

Low Carb Pancakes with Coconut Flour

Low Carb Gluten-Free Low Carb Bread

Coconut Flour Bread

Healthy Bread For All

My Special Keto Hamburger Buns

Easy Grab Breakfast Buns

Tender Keto Seed Bread

Keto Muffin Grab

Keto Twisted Bread

INTRODUCTION

I believe you opened this book because something interest you about the book. I am a bread lover, and my first challenge of being on the keto diet was missing the taste of bread, cookies, muffins and all those lovely sweet dessert treats.

I want you to understand that being on ketogenic diet does not mean deprivation from eating less tasty meals or a sentence to consume meals that taste like poo. Even being on a low carb diet, you can still enjoy that fresh tasty bread, containing a small amount of carbs and only the needed fats.

This book comprise of many traditional recipes from all around the world. Mostly made with gluten -free flours like coconut and almond flour.

If you love to eat bread and also love to eat healthy, then This Keto bread recipe cookbook is put together for people like you who are on a keto diet but lovers of bread and not just bread alone, muffins, buns, cookies, snacks, and sweet and savory dessert meal; all these you can eat and still avoid consuming a lots of carbohydrate in your meal.

Low Carb Bread Recipes

Smart Low Carb Bread

Prep time: 5 minutes
Cook Time: 40 minutes
Servings: 16 slices

Ingredients:

1/2 tsp of xanthan gum, optional
1 tsp of baking powder you can use no aluminum
2/3 cup of coconut flour
1 1/3 cup of almond flour
6 large eggs
3 tbsp of coconut oil
1/2 tsp of salt
1/2 cup of melted butter

Preparations:

1. Crack the eggs open into bowl, then pour into the food processor and blend until finely combined.
2. Combine other ingredients in a bowl and pour into the processor, process until it forms a dough.
3. Greased a 9×5 inch loaf pan, pour in the dough and spread.
4. Place in oven and bake about 40 minutes at 350F until top is browned.

Nutrition facts: 1 serving Calories 145g; Total Fat 13g; Carbohydrates 1g; Protein 4g.

Ketogenic Simple bread

Prep time: 5 minutes

Cook Time: 40 minutes

Servings: 16 slices

Ingredients:

1/2 teaspoon Salt

1/2 teaspoon xanthan gum

2 Cups (200g) of Almond Meal

1 (5g) of teaspoon baking powder

7 Large (50g) Eggs

2 tbsp of (30g) of Coconut Oil

1/2 cup (100g) of melted Butter

Preparations:

1. Heat up the oven to 355 F
2. Crack the eggs open in a bowl and beat on high for 1 to 2 mins.
3. Pour in the melted butter and coconut oil and keep beating.
4. Pour in the remaining ingredients, beat until well combined.
5. Transfer the batter into a baking paper lined loaf pan.
6. Place in the oven and bake about 45 minutes until a skewer inserted in the middle comes out dry.

Nutrition facts:1 serving Calories 234g; Total Fat 23g; Carbohydrates 1g; Protein 14g.

Low Carb Gluten Free Cinnamon Bread
Prep time: 10 minutes
Cook Time: 50 minutes
Servings: 12 slices
Ingredients:
Cinnamon Mix
1 tsps. of cinnamon
1 tbsp of Pyure all-purpose
Bread Batter
1 tsp. of vanilla extract
7 large eggs
3 tbsp of coconut oil liquefied
1/2 cup of butter melted
1/2 tsp of cinnamon
1 tsp of baking powder
1/2 cup of erythritol
1/4 tsp of stevia extract powder
1/2 tsp of salt
1/2 tsp of xanthan gum
1/3 cup of coconut flour
2/3 cup of almond flour
Preparations:
1. Heat up the oven to 350 F

2. Line parchment paper or grease a 9x5 loaf pan.

3. Combine 1 teaspoon of cinnamon and 1 tbsp of Pyure all-purpose in a bowl. Set aside.

4. Combine cinnamon, baking powder, erythritol, stevia, salt, xanthan gum, coconut flour, and almond flour in a separate medium bowl. Set aside.

5. Process vanilla extract, eggs, coconut oil and butter in a food processor until finely combined. Pour in the dry ingredients, process for a few minutes until it forms a batter.

6. Scoop out half cup of the batter and stir into the cinnamon mixture.

7. Pour and spread half measure of the batter onto the loaf pan evenly.

8. Spread the cinnamon mix in half on the batter.

9. Spread the last half of the batter over cinnamon mixture.

10. Spread over the last half of the cinnamon mixture and swirl.

11. Place in the oven and bake for 40 minutes at 350F, then lower the temperature to 325F.You can cover with foil tent if top is turning too brown. Bake more about 15 minutes.

12. Let sit about 5 to 10 minutes in oven until a skewer inserted in the center comes out clean.

Nutrition facts:1 serving Calories 174g; Total Fat 17g; Carbohydrates 3g; Protein 5g.

Keto Gluten Free Gingerbread Bread Loaf

Prep time: 10 minutes

Cook Time: 40 minutes

Servings: 12 slices

Ingredients:

BREAD:

3 eggs

3/4 cups of Sukrin Gold

1/2 cup of butter softened plus 2 tablespoons

1/4 cup of brewed coffee

1 tsp of blackstrap molasses

1/4 tsp of ground nutmeg

1 tsp of cinnamon

1 1/2 tsp of ground ginger

1/4 tsp of baking soda

1/4 tsp of salt

1 tsp of baking powder

1/4 cup of coconut flour

1 cup of almond flour

FROSTING:

1/2 cup of Sukrin Melis or preferred powdered sweetener

1 tbsp of heavy cream

1 tsps of vanilla extract

1 tbsp of softened butter

2 Oz of softened cream cheese

Preparations:

Bread:

1. Heat up the oven to 350°F. Line parchment paper over an 8x4-inch bread pan or grease.

2. Combine the nutmeg, cinnamon, ginger, baking soda, salt, baking powder, coconut flour and almond flour in medium bowl.

3. In a separate bowl, whisk the hot coffee and molasses together.

4. Make the butter creamy by beating it with an electric mixer in a large mixing bowl. Add the Sukrin Gold and beat to blend.

5. Beat in the eggs, one at a time then stir in the coffee mixtures and flour gently until well combined.

6. Transfer the batter into the bread pan and smoothen.

7. Place in the preheated oven and bake until center is set, about 35-40 minutes.

Frosting:

9. Beat butter and cream cheese together until totally combined.

10. Add in the powdered sweetener gently until you have a smooth mixture. Beat in the heavy cream and vanilla. Spread the frosting over bread.

Nutrition facts:1 serving Calories 202g; Total Fat 18g; Carbohydrates 5g; Protein 5g.

Slow cooker Zucchini Bread - Gluten Free

Prep time: 10 minutes

Cook Time: 3 hrs.

Servings: 12 slices

Ingredients

1/2 cup of chopped walnuts

2 cups of zucchini shredded

2 tsp of vanilla

1/2 cup Pyure all purpose

1/3 cup of butter

3 eggs

1/2 tsp of xanthan gum, optional

1/2 tsp of salt

1/2 tsp of baking soda

1 1/2 tsp of baking powder

2 tsps of cinnamon

1/3 cup of coconut flour

1 cup of almond flour

Preparations:

1. Line parchment paper over an 8x4-inch bread pan or grease an 8x4-inch bread pan.

2. Mix together baking soda, baking powder, cinnamon, coconut flour, almond flour, xanthan gum (optional) and salt. Set aside.

3. Combine vanilla, sugar, oil and eggs in a separate large bowl until finely blended.
4. Combine the wet mixture with the dry ingredients.
5. Add in chopped nuts and shredded zucchini.
6. Pour the batter into prepared pan and spread out.
7. Arrange pan on a rack in the crock pot or place crumpled aluminum foil in the crock pot to give a gap of half inch from the bottom.
8. With the lid on, cook for about 3 hours on high.
9. When it's completely cool. Wrap in foil and place in the refrigerator. Best served cold.

Nutrition facts:1 serving Calories 147g; Total Fat 15g; Carbohydrates 6g; Protein 5g.

Cinnamon Rhubarb Gluten Free Muffins
Prep time: 10 minutes
Cook Time: 20 mins
Servings: 12 muffins
Ingredients:
MUFFINS:
1 cup of diced rhubarb
1/8 tsp of Sweet Leaf stevia drops
1/2 tsp of vanilla extract
2 large eggs
4 tbsp of melted butter, unsalted
1/2 cup of sour cream
1/4 tsp of kosher salt
1/4 tsp of baking soda
1 tsp of cinnamon
1 1/2 tsp of baking powder
1/4 cup of Swerve
1/4 cup of coconut flour

3/4 cup of almond flour

TOPPING

1/4 tsp of ground cinnamon

1 1/2 tbsp of Swerve

Preparations:

1. Heat up the oven to 400°F. Grease or line 12 muffin pan.

2. Mix baking soda, cinnamon, coconut flour, baking powder, granular sweetener, almond flour, and salt together in large bowl.

3. Whisk vanilla, eggs, butter, sour cream, and stevia together in medium bowl until smooth.

4. Combine the dry mix with the sour cream mixture, stir until it forms thick batter.

5. Stir in rhubarb

6. Share batter evenly among the muffin cups.

7. Mix the topping ingredients together in bowl.

8. Sprinkle each muffin with half tsp of the sweetened cinnamon mix.

9. Place in the preheated oven and bake about 20 minutes until muffins are browned and skewer inserted in the middle comes out clean.

10. Let muffins cool for 10-15 minutes on the rack. Serve warm.

Nutrition facts:1 serving Calories 104g; Total Fat 9g; Carbohydrates 4g; Protein 2.7g.

Keto, Paleo Quick Gluten Free English Muffin

Prep time: 1 minutes

Cook Time: 1 mins

Servings: 2

Ingredients:

1/4 tsp of baking powder

1 tbs of coconut flour

1 egg at room temperature

1 1/2 tbs of almond butter

1 1/2 tsp of softened coconut oil

1/8 tsp of salt

Preparations:

1. Stir egg, almond butter, and coconut oil together in a bowl until finely combined.

2. Stir in, baking powder, coconut flour and salt.

3. Place in the microwave for 1 minute to 1 1/2 minutes on high.

4. Retrieve muffin and slice in half.

Nutrition facts: 1 serving: Calories 146g;Total Fat 12g; Total Carbohydrates 4g; Protein 5g.

Easy Low Carb French toast

Prep time: 5 minutes
Cook Time: 10 mins
Servings: 16

Ingredients:

1 tsp of cinnamon
1/2 tsp of vanilla extract
2 tbsp of almond milk
Sugar free pancake syrup
2 eggs
1 basic low carb bread, slices into desired thickness

Preparations:

1. Whisk almond milk, vanilla and eggs together in pie pan.
2. Gently whisk in cinnamon.
3. Immerse each bread slices in the egg mixture
4. Grill or cook on hot skillet until browned on both sides.
5. Serve with sugar free pancake syrup

Nutrition facts: Calories 155g; Total Fat 14g; Carbohydrates 3g; Protein 5g.

Low Carb Pancakes – Gluten Free

Prep time: 10 minutes

Cook Time: 10 mins

Servings: 4

Ingredients:

1 tbsp of low carb sweetener

1 tsp of baking powder

1/4 tsp of salt

2 tbsp of oil

1/4 cup of water

2 eggs

1 cup of almond flour

Preparations:

1. Combine the ingredients together.

2. Pour the batter, about 2 to 3 tbsp for a single pancake in hot skillet Cook on both sides until brown.

Once one side is brown underneath and edges are dry, flip over and cook the other side.

Nutrition facts: Calories 255g; Total Fat 23g; l Carbohydrates 3g; Protein 9g.

Microwave Coconut Flour Pumpkin Mug Cake

Prep time: 1 minute

Cook Time: 1 minute

Servings: 2

Ingredients:

1/2 tsp of pumpkin pie spice

1/4 tsp of Sweet Leaf stevia drops

1/2 tsp of vanilla extract

1/4 tsp of baking powder

1 egg beaten

2 tbsp of coconut flour

2 tbsp of pumpkin puree

Preparations:

1. Blend all the ingredients with a fork in a coffee cup.

2. Microwave 1 minutes 30 seconds on high about until a skewer inserted into the middle comes out dry.

3. Serve while it's warm, top with whipped cream. You can add a little low carb milk like coconut or almond if you feel the muffin is too dry.

Nutrition facts: Calories 71g; Total Fat 3g; Carbohydrates 3g; Protein 3g.

Gluten Free Zucchini Apple Fritter Bread

Prep time: 10 minutes
Cook Time: 1 hour 20 minutes
Servings: 12 slices

Ingredients:

1 medium peeled, seeded and chopped zucchini
1/2 cup of almond milk, unsweetened
1/2 tsps of xanthan gum optional
2 tsps of baking powder
1/2 cup of coconut flour
1 cup of almond flour
2 tsps of apple extract
3 eggs
1/2 cup of softened butter
1/2 cup of granular sweetener
1 tsp of cinnamon
1/4 cup of Sukrin Gold
GLAZE:
2-3 tbsp of heavy cream
1/4 cup of Sukrin Melis

Preparations:

1. Heat up the oven to 350°F. Line a parchment paper over or a grease a 9x5-inch loaf pan.

2. Mix together cinnamon and Sukrin Gold in a bowl.

3. Beat butter and granular sweetener together with an electric mixer in a separate medium bowl until creamy and smooth.

4. One after the other, beat in the eggs until well blended; then add apple extract.

5. Combine baking powder and flours together in medium bowl and sift to remove lumps

6. Combine the creamed butter mixture and the dry mix together, stir until incorporated. Stir in the milk until batter is smooth.

7. Pour 1/2 of the batter into the loaf pan; spread out, add 1/2 zucchini, and 1/2 cinnamon mixture/ Sukrin Gold.

8. Slightly pat in the apple mixture.

9. Pour the reserved 1/2 batter on apple layer, the remaining apple mixture, and cinnamon mixture/ Sukrin Gold.

10. Pat the apples into batter and swirl cinnamon mixture/ Sukrin Gold through apples.

11. Place in the preheated oven and bake for 1 hour to 1 hour 10 minutes or until skewer inserted in the middle comes out clean.

12. To make glaze: mix cream and powdered sweetener together until nicely combined.

13. Allow cooling for 15 minutes then drizzle with glaze.

Nutrition facts: Calories 171g; Total Fat 15g; Carbohydrates 3g; Protein 4g.

Quick Low Carb Bread

Prep time: 5 minutes

Cook Time: 1 hour 5 minutes

Servings: 15 slices

Ingredients:

13.5 fluid oz. water or 1 3/4 cup of milk

1 box of Sukrin Bread Mix

Preparations:

1. Combine both ingredients together and allow for 5 minutes to thicken.

2. Place on parchment paper lined cookie sheet as rolls or bread.

3. Transfer to the oven and bake for 20-25 minutes for rolls and 1 hour for bread.

4. Allow Cooling completely on rack.

5. Preferably stored in a bag and refrigerate. Make warm before serving to have a freshly baked delicious taste.

Nutrition facts: Calories 60g; Total Fat 2g;l Carbohydrates 5g; Protein 6g.

Low Carb smooth Bread

Prep time: 10 minutes
Cook Time: 45 minutes
Servings: 16 slices
Ingredients:
12 oz of softened cream cheese
1/4 cup of butter
4 eggs
2 drops of liquid sucralose or Sweetleaf stevia drops optional
1/4 cup of heavy whipping cream.
1/4 cup of olive oil
1 2/3 cup of zero carb unflavored whey protein
1/2 tsp of salt
1/3 tsp of baking soda
1 tsp of xanthan gum
2 1/2 tsps of baking powder
1/4 tsp of cream of tartar
Preparations:
1. Heat up the oven to 325 F. Grease a 9" x 5" bread pan.
2. Place butter and cream cheese in microwave safe dish and microwave for 60 seconds. Remove and blend with stick blender.
3. Add olive oil, heavy cream, few drops of sweetener and eggs; blend until totally combined.
4. Add all the dry ingredients together in separate bowl, blend to combine.
5. Combine cream cheese mixture and the dry ingredients together, stir thoroughly with spatula. Avoid using hand blender or mixer because it will whip it too much.
6. Pour into the prepared pan and bake for 45 minutes at 325 F, or until brown and golden. If you eating right away and the bread top seems too dry, add melted butter. Let cool, then store in a plastic wrap.

Nutrition facts: Calories 200g; Total Fat 15g; Carbohydrates 1.8g; Protein 10g.

Chef Gluten Free Chocolate Mug Cake

Prep time: 2 minutes
Cook Time: 2 minutes
Servings: 1 person

Ingredients:

Sugar free whipped cream if desired
1 tbsp of sugar free chocolate chips, if desired
10 drops monk fruit extract
10 drops stevia liquid extract
1/2 tsp of vanilla extract
1 tbsp of avocado oil or coconut oil
2 tbsp of almond milk or coconut milk
1 large egg
1 tbsp of unsweetened cocoa powder
2 tbsp of coconut flour

Preparations:

1. Mix cocoa powder and coconut flour together in coffee mug or ramekin.
2. Mix in vanilla extract, egg, avocado oil, sweetener(s) and almond milk until finely combined. Add few chocolate chips, if using.
3. Microwave for 1 1/2 to 2 minutes on high. Allow to cool then top with chocolate chips and sugar free whipped cream if using.

Nutrition facts: Calories 281g; Total Fat 22g; Carbohydrates 7g; Protein 9g.

Large Head Pizza Dough Egg Free

Prep time: 10 minutes

Cook Time: 20 minutes

Servings: 8

Ingredients:

2 tbsp of whole psyllium husks whole or ground

1/2 tsps of salt

1/2 tsps of garlic powder

1/3 cup (35 g) of almond flour

2 tbsp of parmesan cheese grated

2 tsps of cream cheese full fat

8 Oz of finely chopped mozzarella cheese slices full fat

Preparations:

1. Microwave mozzarella cheese in microwave bowl about 1 minute and 30 seconds until melted.

2. Allow cooling a bit, then stir in garlic powder, almond flour, parmesan cheese, cream cheese and salt. Knead using your hands.

3. Add a sprinkle in the psyllium bit by bit, as you keep kneading. You may not be able to make all the ingredients incorporate, no problem.

4. Mold dough into ball on parchment paper then flatten.

5. Trim the edges to form a fine circle, then Place on a parchment paper lined baking sheet.

6. Place in the oven and bake for about 15-20 minutes at 425°F, or until browned.

7. Withdraw from the oven and flip then return to the oven and bake more, about 5 minutes until top is brown.

8. Add other toppings and desired sauce. More cheese if desired.

9. Bake for 5 extra minutes. Place under the broiler for a few minute if you desire a browned top.

Nutrition facts: Calories 161g; Total Fat 9g; Carbohydrates 4g; Protein 9g.

Low Carb Coconut Lime Bread

Prep time: 10 minutes

Cook Time: 55 minutes

Servings: 12 slices

Ingredients:

1 tsp of vanilla extract

3 tbsp of Key lime juice

6 Oz of Greek yogurt

8 eggs or less

3 tbsp of coconut oil liquified

1/2 cup of butter, melted

1 tsp of dried lemon peel or lime peel

1 tsp of baking powder

1/2 cup of low carb sweetener

1/4 tsp of stevia concentrated powder

1/2 tsp of salt

1/2 tsp of xanthan gum

1/3 cup of coconut flour

2/3 of cup almond flour

2/3 cup shredded coconut, unsweetened

Lime zest optional - add for stronger lime flavor

Preparations:

1. Mix dried coconut but reserve 2 tablespoons, baking powder, erythritol, xanthan gum, stevia, salt, coconut flour, almond flour, and dried lemon/lime peel together In medium bowl.

2. Combine vanilla extract, lime juice, yogurt, eggs, coconut oil, and butter in a food processor and process until finely combined.

3. Pour in the dry ingredients and process more until batter is incorporated.

4. Spread the finely incorporated batter into a greased loaf pan (9×5 inch).

5. Place in the oven and bake for 15 minutes at 350F, then sprinkle with the remaining coconut on top. Bake for 55 extra minutes or until toothpick inserted comes out dry and top is browned.

Nutrition facts: Calories 242g; Total Fat 23g; Carbohydrates 4g; Protein 4g.

Keto Peanut Flour Bread Gluten Free

Prep time: 10 minutes

Cook Time: 1 hour

Servings: 12 slices

Ingredients:

1 tsps of baking powder

2 tsps of xanthan gum (optional)

1 1/3 cups of peanut flour

1 tsp of vanilla extract

5 eggs

3/4 cup of low carb sweetener

4 oz of cream cheese

1/2 cup of butter

Preparations:

1. Heat up the oven to 350 F. Lightly grease loaf pan.

2. Beat cream cheese and butter together until fluffy. Beat in the eggs one after another. Mix in the vanilla extract.

3. Combine baking powder, xanthan gum, and peanut flour. Slowly beat the flour mix into the butter mix.

4. Spread the batter onto the prepared pan.

5. Place in the preheated oven and bake until skewer inserted in center comes out clean and golden brown, about 50-60 minutes. Let cool for 10 minute, before removing from pan then let cool completely on rack.

Nutrition facts: Calories 152g; Total Fat 13g; Carbohydrates 3g; Protein 7g.

Special Low Carb Garlic Bread Sticks

Prep time: 10 minutes

Cook Time: 15 minutes

Servings: 6

Ingredients:

1/4 cup of butter melted

2 large eggs

1-1/2 cups of mozzarella grated

1/2 tsp o xanthan gum optional

1/2 tsp of salt

1/2 tsp of garlic powder

2 tsp of baking powder

2 tbsp of coconut flour

3 tbsp of unflavored whey protein powder

1 cup of almond flour plus extra for kneading dough

Topping:

1/2 tsp of garlic powder

2 tbsp of grated parmesan cheese

3 tbsp of softened butter

Preparations:

Bread:

1. Heat up the oven to 400°F.

2. Whisk xanthan gum, garlic powder, baking powder, coconut flour, whey protein, salt and almond flour together in a large bowl.

3. In a microwave safe bowl, melt mozzarella in microwave.

4. Stir dry mix, butter, eggs into mozzarella until it forms dough. You can microwave dough ball about 5 to 10 seconds at high if cheese begins to firm in other to get all ingredients blended into dough. You can also add almond flour as necessary in case the dough is sticky.

5. Between two sheets of parchment paper arrange the dough ball, then roll dough out into a circle using rolling pin about 1/4 inch thick.

6. Remove the upper parchment paper, then Place dough onto baking sheet. Slice dough into stick pieces using a knife or pizza cutter.

Topping:

7. Combine the topping ingredients in a bowl, then and spread on the sliced dough.

8. Place in the oven and bake for 10 to 15 minutes or until top begins to brown. Serve warm.

Nutrition facts: Calories 425g; Total Fat 33g; Carbohydrates 4.6g; Protein 24g.

Fancy Pepperoni Pizza Muffins

Prep time: 10 minutes
Cook Time: 30 minutes
Servings: 12 muffins

Ingredients:

1 cup of shredded mozzarella cheese, divided
1/2 cup of mini pepperoni
5 eggs beaten
3 tbsp of water
1/2 tsp of salt
1 tsp of baking powder
2/3 cup of almond flour
1/4 cup of coconut flour
1/2 cup of Asiago cheese shredded
5 oz of cream cheese

Preparations:

1. Heat up the oven to 400°F. Grease or Spray muffin molds.
2. Combine almond flour, coconut flour, grated Asiago cheese, cream cheese, baking powder, beaten egg, water, and salt In large mixing bowl.
3. Mix in 1/2 cup mozzarella cheese and pepperoni.
4. Pour muffin cups about 3/4 measure full.
5. Sprinkle with more half cup of mozzarella cheese on top.
6. Place in the preheated oven and bake for 25-30 minutes or until muffins are lightly browned and firm.
7. Served warm, at room temperature, or store in refrigerator.

Nutrition facts: Calories 182g; Total Fat 14g; Carbohydrates 3.6g; Protein 7.8g.

Cranberry Bread Gluten Free

Prep time: 10 minutes

Cook Time: 1 hour 15 minutes

Servings: 12

Ingredients:

1 bag (12 ounces) of cranberries

1/2 cup of coconut milk

4 large eggs at room temperature

1 tsp of blackstrap molasses optional

4 tbsp of no-salt melted butter or coconut oil

1 tsp of salt

1/2 tsp of baking soda

1 1/2 tsp of baking powder

1/2 tsp of stevia powder

1/2 cup of powdered erythritol or Swerve

2 cups of almond flour

Preparations:

1. Heat up the oven to 350 F. Line parchment paper or grease a 9 x 5 inch loaf pan.

2. Whisk the baking soda, flour, baking powder, stevia, salt and erythritol together in a bowl; set aside.

3. Combine coconut milk, eggs, molasses and butter in a different bowl.

4. Combine wet and dry mixture, mix until nicely incorporated.

5. Gently mix in cranberries.

6. Spread the batter into prepared loaf pan.

7. Place in the oven and bake about 1 hour and 15 minutes or until a skewer inserted in the middle comes clean.

8. Let cool on a wire rack about 15 minutes before removing from pan.

Nutrition facts: Calories 179g; Total Fat 15g; Carbohydrates 4.7g; Protein 7g.

Cheese Muffins and Bacon Egg

Prep time: 10 minutes

Cook Time: 30 minutes

Servings: 12

Ingredients:

1/2 cup of shredded cheddar cheese

3 strips of bacon, crispy cook with no sugar, fat discard, then crumbled

5 eggs beaten

3 tbsp of water

1/2 tsp of salt

1 tsp of baking powder

2/3 cup of almond flour

1/4 cup of coconut flour

1/2 cup of grated parmesan cheese

2/3 cup of cottage cheese

Preparations:
1. Heat up the oven to 400 F. Prepare the muffin cups by greasing it; set aside.
2. Combine beaten egg, baking powder, almond meal, coconut flour, salt, parmesan cheese water, and cottage cheese in mixing bowl.
3. Mix in cheddar cheese and crumbled bacon.
4. Pour the mix into the prepared muffin cups 3/4 full. Add a sprinkle of shredded cheddar cheese over the top, if desired.
5. Place in the preheated oven and bake about 25 to 30 minutes, until muffins are lightly browned and firm.

Nutrition facts: Calories 197g; Total Fat 14g; Carbohydrates 2g; Protein 15g.

All the way Low Carb Bread
Prep time: 5 minutes
Cook Time: 45 minutes
Servings: 8
Ingredients:
1 cup of shredded summer squash
1/4 tsp of ground nutmeg
1 1/2 tsp of ground cinnamon
1 1/2 tsp of baking powder
6 tbsp of coconut flour
1 cup plus 2 tbsp of almond flour
1 tsp of sugar-free vanilla extract
2 tbsp of vegetable oil
1/4 cup of butter melted
1/2 cup of Swerve
2 eggs beaten
Preparations:
1. Heat up the oven to 325 degrees F. Prepare an 8×4 inch loaf pan by greasing it.
2. Beat the eggs an electric mixer until fluffy in a large bowl; beat in the vanilla, oil, butter, and sugar
3. Mix in the nutmeg, cinnamon, baking powder, and flour(s) in separate bowl. Add the dry ingredients slowly into egg mixture.
4. Gradually mix in the squash.

5. Spread over the prepared loaf pan.
6. Place in the prepared oven and bake about 45 minutes or until a skewer inserted in the middle comes out dry.

Nutrition facts: Calories 154g; Total Fat 14g; Carbohydrates 2g; Protein 5g.

Special Keto Low Carb Crackers

Prep time: 10 minutes

Cook Time: 15 minutes

Servings: 6

Ingredients:

1 tbsp of whole psyllium husks or flax meal

1 tbsp of coconut oil

2 tbsp of water

3/4 tsp of sea salt to taste

2 tbsp of sunflower seeds

1 cup of almond flour

Preparations:

1. Heat up the oven to 350°F.
2. Blend psyllium, almond flour, sea salt and sunflower seeds together in a food processor, and pulse in coconut oil and water until it forms a dough.
3. Inside two sheets of parchment paper, Place the dough ball, then force down to flatten. Roll dough into a thickness of about 1/10 to 1/16 inch.
4. Discard the top parchment paper, place on cutting board, then slice into 1-inch squares with a knife or a pizza cutter. Top with sprinkle of sea salt if desired.
5. Set the sliced dough on a baking sheet and bake until edges are crisp and brown and at 350°F. Allow cooling on a rack before separating into squares.

Nutrition facts: Calories 151g; Total Fat 13g; Carbohydrates 3g; Protein 4g.

Ketogenic Baked Cucumber Chips

Prep time: 10 minutes

Cook Time: 10 hours

Servings: 6

Ingredients:

2 medium cucumbers

1/2 tsp of sea salt or more

2 tsp of apple cider vinegar

1 tbsp of avocado or olive oil

Preparations:

1. For a best result I recommend using a mandolin slicer to slice cucumber very thin.

2. Discard any excess moisture from cucumber slices with a paper towel.

3. Toss cucumber slices, vinegar, oil and salt together in a large bowl.

4. Oven method: Arrange cucumber slices on baking tray lined with parchment paper. Dry for 3-4 hours at 175°F or until crispy.

5. Dehydrator method: Arrange cucumber slices on trays and dry for 10-12 hours at 125-135°F or until crispy.

6. Allow cooling before serving.

Don't slice the cucumbers too thin if using pans lined with foil and flip over about half-way into cooking for easy removal.

Nutrition facts: Calories 25g; Total Fat 2g; Carbohydrates 1g; Protein 0g.

Quick Radish Chips

Prep time: 10 minutes

Cook Time: 10 minutes

Servings: 4

Ingredients:

1/2 tsp of coarse kosher or sea salt

16 ounces of radishes

Oil for deep frying best use palm oil

Preparations:

1. Heat 2 to 3 inches oil to 325°F in a heavy saucepan or deep fat fryer.

2. Slice the radishes into thinly slices using a sharp knife or mandoline slicer.

3. Arrange radishes in pot, pour in water to cover. Boil for 4 to 5 minutes over high heat or until skins lighten and radish are translucent. Place radish slices in seiva to drain.

4. Fry the radish in the hot oil until they turn a deep golden brown, about 8 to 10 minutes .Use paper towels to drain then season with salt.

Nutrition facts: Calories 48g; Total Fat 4.7g; Carbohydrates 1g; Protein 0.8g.

Eggs Free Gluten Free Pumpkin Cookies

Prep time: 10 minutes

Cook Time: 10 minutes

Servings: 30 cookies

Ingredients:

1/2 cup of low carb sweetener

1/4 cup of hot water

1 tbsp of grass-fed gelatin

2 tbsp of water

1/2 tsp of vanilla extract

1/2 cup pumpkin puree

1/4 cup of coconut oil

1/2 tsp of sea salt

1/8 tsp of cloves

1/4 tsp of ginger

1/2 tsp of cinnamon
1/2 tsp of baking powder
1/2 tsp of baking soda
Coconut flour (1/4 cup)
1 cup almond flour

Preparations:

1. In small bowl, combine baking powder, cinnamon, baking soda, coconut flour, almond flour, sea salt cloves, and ginger.
2. In a separate bowl, combine vanilla extract, pumpkin puree and coconut oil.
3. In a separate mixing bowl, Pour 2 tbsp of water and add gelatin. Let sit for 5 minutes.
4. Pour in quarter cup of hot water into the gelatin mix and whisk to dissolve the gelatin completely. Add low carb sweetener and beat until mixture is fluffy.
5. Slowly mix in the pumpkin mixture then mix with an electric mixer to combine finely.
6. Fold the dry ingredients into the pumpkin mix
7. Drop mixture onto a lined or greased baking pans. Use your finger to Press down slightly.
8. Place in the oven and bake for 12 to 15 minutes at 350°F. Let cookies cool completely, then remove from pan.

Nutrition facts: Calories 43g; Total Fat 3g; Carbohydrates 1g; Protein 1g.

No Egg Coconut Flour Cookies

Prep time: 10 minutes
Cook Time: 9 minutes
Servings: 16 cookies

Ingredients:

2 tablespoons of Choc Zero Honest Syrup
Pinch of sea salt
1/4 cup of ghee butter
6 tablespoons of coconut flour

Preparations:

Heat up the oven to 365 F

1. Combine every ingredients into a food processor and pulse to form a dough.
2. Share dough evenly into 16 balls and place them on a baking pan lined with parchment paper. Press down to flatten into cookies shape.
3. Place in the preheated oven and bake for 7 to 9 minutes or until edges are brown.

Nutrition facts: Calories 101g; Total Fat 9g; Carbohydrates 2g; Protein 1g.

Low Carb Keto Hazelnut Flour Cookies

Prep time: 15 minutes
Cook Time: 25 minutes
Servings: 20 cookies

Ingredients:

1 tablespoon of powdered erythritol
Crushed hazelnuts to garnish
1 teaspoon of vanilla
10 drops of vanilla stevia glycerite
2 egg whites
1 cup (90g) of hazelnut meal ground hazelnuts

Preparations:

1. Beat the egg whites until stiff peaks forms.

2. Gently mix in the vanilla, erythritol, stevia and hazelnut meal until finely blended. Adjust sweetener the way you desire sweetness.

3. Drop dough using a spoon on a parchment paper lined baking sheet. Press down to flatten as desired.

4. Place in the oven and bake for 25 minutes at 320°F or until slightly browned.

5. Allow cooling few minutes, they gradually become firm as they cool.

Nutrition facts: Calories 34.3g; Total Fat 4g; Carbohydrates 0.9g; Protein 1.1g.

Low Carb Cranberry Walnut Cookies

Prep time: 10 minutes

Cook Time: 15 minutes

Servings: 35 cookies

Ingredients:

3/4 cup LC Foods white sweetener - Swerve or erythritol

1/4 cup of chopped walnuts

1/3 cup of dried cranberries (sugar free)

1 large egg room temperature

1/2 cup of room temperature butter

1/2 tsp of ground cinnamon

1 1/2 cups (156g) of almond flour

Preparations:

1. Combine cinnamon and almond flour in bowl

2. Mix sweetener and butter with an electric mixer in large mixing bowl.

3. Gently blend egg into butter mix, gradually mix in the almond flour mix.

4. Mix in the walnuts and cranberries.

5. Spoon the dough onto cookie sheets lined with parchment paper or silicone lined.

6. Place in the oven and bake for 12-15 minutes at 350°F or until cookies edges are brown.

Nutrition facts: Calories 55g; Total Fat 4g; Carbohydrates 3g; Protein 2g.

Gluten Free -Cranberry Biscotti Cookies
Prep time: 5 minutes
Cook Time: 10 minutes
Servings: 14 cookies
Ingredients:
Melted low carb dark chocolate, optional
1/2 cup of sliced almonds
1/2 cup of dried cranberries (sugar free)
1/4 tsp of sea salt
1/2 tsp of baking soda
1/4 cup of coconut flour
1 1/2 cups of almond flour
1/4 tsp of lemon stevia drops and a 1/2 tsp of lemon extract
1/3 cup of low carb sweetener
1 tsp of vanilla
2 eggs
Preparations:
1. Beat the eggs, stevia, Swerve, vanilla and together until frothy using an electric mixer.
2. Combine the baking soda, almond flour, salt and coconut flour in different bowl.
3. Combine wet and dry mixture, stir until it forms dough, and then mix in the almonds and cranberries.
4. Mold dough into a long rectangle on a cookie sheet lined with parchment paper.
5. Place in the oven and bake for about 20 minutes a time 350°F or until browned on top.
6. Withdraw from the oven and leave to completely cool.
7. Cut into slight diagonal thinly sizes.
8. Transfer to the baking pan and bake at 350°F for 15 to 20 minutes until toasted.
9. When it's cool, you can drizzle melted chocolate over the top, if desired.

Nutrition facts: Calories 112g; Total Fat 9g; Carbohydrates 3g; Protein 5g. Each cookie has about 1.9g erythritol

Keto Low Carb Hamburger Buns

Prep time: 10 minutes

Cook Time: 30 minutes

Servings: 15 buns

Ingredients:

Sesame seeds, if desired

2 tbsp of apple cider vinegar

3/4 cup of egg whites

1 cup of hot water

1/2 tsp of sea salt

1/3 cup of whole psyllium husks

1/4 cup coconut flour

1 1/2 tsp of baking soda

1 cup of almond flour

Preparations:

1. Heat up the oven to 350°F. Line parchment paper over a baking pan.

2. In a medium bowl, combine baking soda, psyllium, coconut flour almond flour, and sea salt. Set aside.

3. Stir together hot water, egg whites, and apple cider in large mixing bowl.

4. Mix in the dry into the wet mixture. It gradually thicken while it sits. When thickened enough, divide into 15 different pieces.

5. Mold each piece (best use wet hands) into a bun.

6. Transfer to the prepared baking pan bake until centers are set and edges are browned, about 25 to 30 minutes.

7. Allow to cool for 10 to 15 minutes on rack, remove from the baking pan and set on the rack to completely cool.

Nutrition facts: Calories 77g; Total Fat 3; Carbohydrates 2g; Protein 3g.

Keto, Paleo Low Carb Hamburger Buns Recipe

Prep time: 10 minutes
Cook Time: 25 minutes
Servings: 12 buns

Ingredients:

1/4 cup of Coconut oil
1/2 cup of Avocado oil
2 large eggs
2 cup of egg whites
3/4 teaspoon of Sea salt
1 1/2 teaspoon of Baking soda
1 cup (112 grams) of Coconut flour
3/4 cup of Warm water
6 tablespoon (27 grams) of Whole psyllium husks

Preparations:

1. Heat up the oven to 350 Grease a muffin top pan.
2. Mix water and psyllium in bowl, set aside.
3. Pour the remaining ingredients into a mixing bowl or a food processor, blend using an electric mixer or pulse until finely combined.
4. Pour psyllium gel into mixing bowl or the food processor, blend using an electric mixer or pulse until blended.
5. Divide and smoothen batter into 12 equal muffin top molds.
6. Place in the preheated oven and bake for 25 to 30 minutes or until skewer inserted in the center comes out clean and edges are brown.
7. Allow sitting in pan about 10 to 15 minutes. Remove bread and let completely cool on rack.

Nutrition facts: Calories 198g; Total Fat 8; Carbohydrates 2g; Protein 8g.

Low Carb Keto Bread

Prep time: 10 minutes

Cook Time: 21 minutes

Servings: 12

Ingredients:

3 large eggs

1 tablespoon of baking powder

1 cup (46 grams) of crushed pork rinds

1/4 cup (27 grams) of parmesan cheese grated

2 cups (210 grams) of mozzarella cheese grated

8 oz of cream cheese

Spices and herbs to taste, if desired

Preparations:

1. Heat up the oven to 375°F. Line parchment paper over baking sheet.

2. Microwave mozzarella and cream cheese for one minute in a microwaveable on high power, stir and microwave more for another minute and stir again until the cheese is fully melted.

3. Stir in egg, baking powder, pork rinds, and parmesan until totally incorporated.

4. Pour the mixture onto baking pan lined with parchment paper.

5. Place in the oven and bake for 15 to 20 at 375 F or until top is lightly brown.

6. Allow sitting in pan about 10 to 15 minutes. Remove bread and let it completely cool on rack.

7. Divide into 12 similar pieces. Great as sandwiches or eaten plain.

Nutrition facts: Calories 166g; Total Fat 13g; Carbohydrates 1g; Protein 9g.

Small Chocolate Chip Muffins with Peanut Butter

Prep time: 10 minutes

Cook Time: 12 minutes

Servings: 24

Ingredients:

2 tbsp of butter or coconut oil for dairy-free

1/4 cup of chocolate chips, sugar free

1/3 cup of almond milk or coconut milk

1 large egg

1/3 cup of golden low carb sweetener

1/3 cup of peanut butter

1/4 tsp of salt

1 1/2 tsp of baking powder

1 cup of peanut flour

Preparations:

1. Heat up the oven to 350°F. Grease mini muffin pan or Line with baking cups.

2. In small bowl, combine baking powder, peanut flour, and salt.

3. Beat butter, sweetener and peanut butter together in large mixing bowl, until creamy.

4. Beat in low carb milk and egg until smooth.

5. Combine wet mixture and dry mixture until well blended, then add chocolate chips.

6. Scoop the batter onto the prepared muffin cups.

7. Place in the oven and bake for 10 to 12 minutes.

8. Allow cooling on wire rack about 5 minutes, then remove to completely cool on rack.

Nutrition facts: Calories 131g; Total Fat 10g; Carbohydrates3g; Protein 8g

Low Carb Gluten Free -Garlic Coconut Flour Bagels

Prep time: 5 minutes

Cook Time: 15 minutes

Servings: 6 bagels

Ingredients:

1/2 tsp of baking powder

1/2 tsp of salt

1 1/2 tsp of garlic powder

6 eggs

2 tsp of guar gum if desired

1/2 cup of coconut flour sifted

1/3 cup of melted butter

Preparations:

1. Blend eggs, garlic powder, salt and butter together in a bowl.

2. Combine baking powder, coconut flour with and guar (if desired).Whisk in the coconut flour mix into batter until no lump forms.

3. Scoop the batter into a greased donut pan.

4 Place in the oven and bake for 15 min at 400 F.

5. Allow to completely cool 10 to 15 minutes on rack then remove from pan.

Nutrition facts: Calories 191g; Total Fat 16g; Carbohydrates3g; Protein 8g

Gluten Free -French Toast Bagels

Prep time: 10 minutes

Cook Time: 15 minutes

Servings: 6 bagels

Ingredients:

1/2 tsp of baking powder

1/2 tsp of xanthan gum (optional)

1/2 cup of coconut flour, sifted

1/2 tsp of salt

5-10 drops of stevia glycerite

1 tsp of maple extract

2 tsp of sugar-free vanilla extract

1 tbsp of cinnamon

6 eggs

1/3 cup of melted butter

Preparations:

1. Blend cinnamon, butter, eggs, stevia, maple extract, vanilla extract, and salt together.

2. Combine baking powder, coconut flour and xanthan gum (optional).

3. Whisk dry mixture into wet mixture until no more lump.

4. Scoop batter into a greased donut pan.

5. Place in the oven and bake for 15 minutes at 400 F.

Nutrition facts: Calories 207g; Total Fat 16g; Carbohydrates3g; Protein 8g

Fancy Carrot Cake Cream Cheese Muffins- Low Carb

Prep time: 15 minutes
Cook Time: 25 minutes
Servings: 12

Ingredients:

1/4 cup of chopped pecans
1 tsp of cinnamon
1 tsp of allspice
1/4 cup of oil
1/4 cup of almond milk
1/2 tsp of baking powder
3/4 cup of carrots
1/2 cup of oat fiber
 1/2 cup of almond flour
1/4 tsp of stevia extract powder
1/4 cup of powdered erythritol or Swerve
1 tsp of cream of tartar
4 eggs

Filling:

1/2 tsp of vanilla extract
8 oz of cream cheese
1/4 cup of powdered erythritol or Swerve
1/4 teaspoon of stevia extract powder
1 tbsp of coconut flour
1 egg

Preparations:

1. Grease 12 muffin pans
1. Separate egg whites from the yolks Beat cream of tartar and the egg whites until it forms stiff peaks.
2. Stir the egg yolks, carrot, cinnamon, allspice, oil, almond milk, oat fiber, almond flour stevia and erythritol in a separate bowl until well combined.
3. Carefully mix in pecans and egg whites.
4. Spread the batter equally into the prepared 12 muffin pan.

Filling:

5. Beat egg and cream cheese, erythritol, stevia, coconut flour and vanilla until finely blended.
6. Pour a few teaspoons on each muffin.
7. Place in the oven and bake for 20-25 minutes at 350ºF.

Nutrition facts: Calories 160g; Total Fat 14g; Carbohydrates2g; Protein 5g

Low Carb Pancakes with Coconut Flour
Prep time: 10 minutes
Cook Time: 10 minutes
Servings: 12 pancakes
Ingredients:
3 eggs plus 1 more if batter is too thick
Water if needed
1/2 tsp of baking powder
1/4 cup of coconut flour
1/2 tsp of vanilla extract
1/4 tsp of salt or more
1 packet of stevia
1/4 cup of heavy cream or sour cream
1/4 cup of unsalted butter melted
Preparations:
1. Whisk vanilla extract, eggs, stevia, cream salt, and butter together.
2. Combine baking powder and coconut flour in separate bowl.
3. Mix dry and wet ingredients together.
4. Allow batter sit for few minutes to thicken. Add egg or heavy cream or water if batter is too thick.
5. Pour oil into a pan and heat over medium high. Scoop batter onto skillet.
6. Cook pancakes until set.

Nutrition facts: Calories 77g; Total Fat 7g; Carbohydrates 1g; Protein 1g

Low Carb Gluten-Free Low Carb Bread

Prep time: 5 minutes

Cook Time: 40 minutes

Servings: 12 slices

Ingredients:

1/2 tsp of xanthan gum optional

1 tsp of whole psyllium husks

2 tsp of baking powder

1/3 cup of coconut flour

2/3 cup of sesame seed flour

6 eggs

3 tsp of liquified coconut oil

1/2 tsp of salt

1/2 cup of melted butter

Preparations:

1. Greased a 9×5 inch loaf pan.

2. Crack eggs open then blend in the food processor until well combined.

3. Pour in the rest ingredients and process until it forms a dough.

4. Pour dough into the prepared loaf pan.

5. Place in the oven and bake for 40 minutes at 350F or until top is browned.

Nutrition facts: Calories 146g; Total Fat 13g; Carbohydrates 1.2g; Protein 3.5g

Coconut Flour Bread

Prep time: 5 minutes

Cook Time: 55 minutes

Servings: 15 slices

Ingredients:

1/4 cup of melted coconut oil

1/2 cup of olive oil

2 large eggs see note

1 pint egg whites 2 cups

3/4 tsp of sea salt

1 1/2 of teaspoons baking soda

1 cup coconut flour 125g

3/4 cup of warm water

6 tbsp. of finely grind whole psyllium husks

Preparations:

1. Heat up the oven to 350°F.

2. Grease or line parchment paper over pan.

3. Pulse ingredients in a food processor until nicely incorporated or mix with an electric mixer.

4. Pour and smoothen the batter into the prepared loaf pan.

5. Place in the oven and bake for 45-55 minutes or until skewer inserted comes out clean and edges are brown.

6. Allow bread sit for 15 minutes in pan. Remove from pan and let cooling on rack completely.

Nutrition facts: Calories 127g; Total Fat 13g; Carbohydrates 1.9g; Protein 3g

Healthy Bread For All

Prep time: 10 mins

Cook time: 30 mins

Servings: 10

Ingredients:

1 tablespoon of apple cider vinegar

1 teaspoon of sweetener

1/4 cup of coconut oil

5 eggs

1/4 teaspoon of salt

1/4 cup of ground flaxseed meal

 2 tablespoons of coconut flour

1 1/2 cups almond flour

1 1/2 tsp of baking soda

Preparations:

1. Preheat oven to 350F

2. Add baking soda, flax, coconut flour, almond flour and salt in a food processor; Process, add in the eggs, vinegar and oil then process.

3. Transfer the batter into a greased loaf pan.

4. Bake for 30 minutes at 350 degrees

Nutritional per servings: 2 slices per servings: 189 Calories,16g Fat, 7g Protein, 6g Carbohydrate.

My Special Keto Hamburger Buns

Prep Time: 15 mins

Cook time: 20 mins

Servings: 10

Ingredients:

1 tablespoon of olive oil

1/4 cup of water

1/2 teaspoon of garlic powder

5 eggs, beaten

1/2 teaspoon of onion powder

1 teaspoon of baking powder

2 1/2 teaspoons of dill weed

3/4 cup of cottage cheese

1 tablespoon of sugar substitute, or to taste

2 cups of flax seed meal

1 teaspoon of salt

Preparations:

1. Preheat oven to 350 degrees F. Lightly grease a baking pan or line with parchment paper.

2. Mix onion powder, garlic powder, baking powder, salt, dill weed sugar substitute, and flax seed meal together in a bowl. Stir in oil, water, cottage cheese, and eggs until well and no visible strings of egg white. Let batter rest for 2 to 3 minutes until thickened a bit.

3. Spread batter into a rectangle with 1 to 2 inches from the edges of the prepared pan.

4. Place in the preheated oven and bake, about 20 minutes until the top springs back when pressed browned. Allow to cool before slicing.

Nutrition Per Serving: 7.6 g carbohydrates; 182 calories; 9.1 g protein; 13.8 g fat; 84 mg cholesterol; 388 mg sodium

Easy Grab Breakfast Buns

Prep Time: 15 mins

Cook time: 25 mins

Servings: 4

Ingredients:

1 teaspoon of baking powder

½ cup of sour cream

2 eggs

2 tablespoons of olive oil

½ teaspoon of salt

2 tablespoons of psyllium husk powder

1 tablespoon of sunflower seeds (shelled)

1 tablespoon of whole flax seeds

¾ cup of almond flour

Preparations:

1. Preheat oven to 400F degrees.

2. Mix baking powder, psyllium, seeds, almond flour and salt in a bowl.

3. Carefully mix in the sour cream, olive oil and eggs.

4. Dough might be a bit sticky, allow sitting for 5 minutes.

5. Moist hand and divide the dough into 4 pieces, shaping dough to form a circle, one after another.
6. Line parchment paper over a cake pan, and then place the dough.
7. Transfer to the oven and bake for 20-25 minutes until browned.

Nutrition per Serving: 8.66 carbohydrate; 309 calories, 26g fat, 9.4g protein. Dietary fiber.

Tender Keto Seed Bread

Prep Time: 5 mins
Cook time: 45 mins
Servings: 20

Ingredients:

1 tablespoon of poppy seeds or sesame seeds
¾ cup of heavy whipping cream
½ cup of melted butter or melted coconut oil
7 ounces of cream cheese
6 eggs
1 teaspoons of salt
3 teaspoons of baking powder
¼ cup of ground psyllium husk powder
½ cup of flaxseed
51/3 tablespoon of sesame seeds
¾ cup of coconut flour
1 cup of almond flour
1 teaspoon of ground fennel seeds or ground caraway seeds

Preparations:

1. Preheat the oven to 350°F.
2. with the exemption of sesame seeds or poppy seeds. Combine all dry ingredients in a bowl, mix thoroughly.
3. Mix the wet ingredients together in a different large bowl until smooth.
4. Combine both ingredients together and mix thoroughly.
5. Line parchment paper over a 4 x 7 inches bread pan and also greased bread pan.

6. Transfer the batter into the greased pan and bake on lower rack in the oven for 45 minutes.

7. Insert a knife into the center of the bread to confirm if its done, its ready if the knife comes out clean.

8. Remove from the oven and place bread on a rack to cool.

9. Slice and enjoy. You can store in the freezer.

Nutrition Per serving: 2g Carbohydrate; 223g Calories; 11g Protein; 20g Fat; 5g Dietary Fiber.

Keto Muffin Grab

Prep Time: 5 min

Cook time: 10 min

Servings: 3

Ingredients:

3 tablespoon of butter or coconut oil, for frying

1 pinch of salt

½ teaspoon of baking powder

2 tablespoon of coconut flour

2 eggs

Preparations:

1. Combine baking powder, coconut flour and salt together in a bowl, mix well.

2. Whisk the eggs into the bowl containing flour mixture; let sit for some mins.

3. Add melted butter and dollops three spoon of batter into a frying pan, on medium high.

4. Fry breads on both sides for 6-10 minutes bake in the oven at 400°F for 10 minutes in a 3 inches greased cupcake tin.

5. Serve with a spread of butter and your desired topping.

Nutrition Per serving: 1g Carbohydrate; 215g Calories; 12g Protein; 15g Fat; 3g Dietary Fiber

Keto Twisted Bread

Prep Time: 5 min

Cook time: 10 min

Servings: 3

Ingredients:

1 egg, for brushing

2 ounces of green pesto

1 egg

22/3 ounces of butter, melted

1½ cups of shredded mozzarella cheese

1 teaspoon of baking powder

½ teaspoon of salt

4 tablespoon of coconut flour

½ cup of almond flour

Preparations:

1. Preheat the oven to 350°F (175°C).

2. Combine the dry ingredients in a medium bowl; stir.

3. Mix cheese and melted butter together in a skillet on low heat. Stir together using a fork to have smooth texture. Crack eggs and stir into the skillet.

4. Stir in dry the ingredients until a dough forms.

5. Arrange two sheets of parchment paper, place the dough between and roll using pin to form a ⅛ inch thick rectangle.

6. Top with pesto and slice into 1-inch strips. Twist dough and set on a parchment paper lined baking sheet; brush the twisted dough with the egg mixture.

7. Transfer in the oven and bake until they're golden brown about 15–20 minutes.

Nutrition Per serving: 1g Carbohydrate; 204g Calories; 7g Protein; 18g Fat; 2g Dietary Fiber

CPSIA information can be obtained
at www.ICGtesting.com
Printed in the USA
LVHW010428010322
712230LV00007B/832